CROW'S FALL

To the memory of my father.

CROW'S FALL
Ivan White

Cape Goliard Press London 1969
in association with
Grossman Publishers New York

S.B.N. Cloth: 206.61667.8
Paper: 206.61668.6
Lib. of Congress No.: 69.17468

Acknowledgements are due to the following: B.B.C. Third Programme – 'The Poet's Voice and Poetry Now' (George MacBeth), The Aylesford Review, Envoi, Extra Verse, Outposts, Poet International Quarterly, Skeletons, Socialist Commentary, The Spectator, Tribune.

The poem 'Mahler' was awarded second prize of £50 in the Guinness Poetry Competition in the Cheltenham Festival, 1964.

'For human natnre, honest human nature
(Which the fear-pampered heart denies)
Knows its own miracle: not to go mad.'

Robert Graves

SECTION 1   *The human nature of myth*

FIRST OFFERING

Grinding his foot
In sand, the child
Spreads patterns to loot
Vague discrepancies.

Twists his shoe, bends
Finger outstretched,
Outlines and amends
His exaggerated art.

He leaves it there
For the sea's whim –
Whether to drown or spare
His first offering.

The force he groped
With, not powered enough,
He looks where nature stooped
To aggravate the small.

Where ants lift their dead,
Hulked on fragile backs,
Lugging an act homeward
Of frail compassion.

The child observes
How insecurity
So stark unnerves
The practical, and learns

How such images crave
Otherwhere than poetry
In which to move,
Strain and grow teeth.

THE INVENTION GAME

The game is that each of us
Attempts to design the
Abstract implement that will
Fit the other's cupped, receptive hands.
It is played with the belief
Of discovering one object
Common to all hands which would
Purposefully occupy them.

The test tube of bacteria
And the tablets of a healing drug
Are found on the same laboratory shelf.
A learned minority
Prescribes their manipulation
Often without understanding.
The avenue with a monopoly of trees
Will usually house the influential
Although the nature of the poplar
From green height dwarfs them.

Some were given rifles with perverse
Instruction on how to minister
To gun metal with more tenderness than was
Ever learnt for their slim, girl wives
Now fallen upon roughly in the
Coarse intervals between bearing.

That jew had a synagogue
Under an architrave of words
Where often he fed spiritually.
The catholic, steeped in idolatry,
Worships beside columns of dead latin
And an expensive Madonna
Which always reassures him.

Self love was tried, but since
This inevitably grew into obsession,
Consummation being impossible,
Pederasty was invented to
Possess the unrequited limbs.

The sane and the normal strike as
Teachers too cold to forge
Sound answers on any mature anvil.
The religious go woolgathering dogma
And have consequently mislaid the thread.
Sincerity is sick with the leaflets of
The long faced who say they are saved.
Even the private birdsong of a personal love
Suffers from the losing efforts to protect
It from the bright vermilion public eyeball.
I have come to believe that,
Since they hold it in their reaching hands,
It was not Prometheus but small children,
Cosy with Jesus, who invented warmth.

SOMETIMES WITHOUT DEDICATION

Sometimes, caught without dedication,
You will be disturbed by the
Rancour of curious disbelief which will
Engage your weaknesses
In pointed derision
And disdain as odd
The outward features of
Your strength and eccentricity.

Sleep will elude you then, the stiff sheet
Yield less easily as the arm threshes
Repelling the stark fear of your gift
For deep singing.
Of the blurred quavers
Chafing your ears you would ask,
'How audible is love?'

Turning you will feel
Her, beside you sleeping,
Place instinctively her
Cool fingers across your
Forehead and you will be calm,
Reminded that there
Exists this intimacy where
In all else you have failed.

DOUBLE SWAN

The swan's head moves like
A curved pincer spliced from its
Twin muscle of body and image.

This way words swim to
Enact or ripple their own atmosphere
In sustained collision,

As a still lake responds
Obediently with facsimile
Of all within range.

The flung sound shocks,
Antagonises, soothes or inducts
Sharply if the pincer mauls flesh.

With partial failure to connect
A wavering is caused so that object
And reflection overlap.

Should no chord be reciprocated,
Words collapse suddenly
As the swan, if shot

In the neck, would fall
Parallel with, then sink
Through its own image.

ATTEMPT AT COMMUNION

Steered over rock as wind
Turns from caves, back over sea,
Love inherits the trapped silence.
The moon installs gentleness
Within the amoeba reach of small waves.
Tentacles of a single cell
Rest from anger. Silver soothes.
The metal of the sea accepts her frail hands' movement.
The reflected pallor of her face
Sets like a steel worker's mask,
Shallow, beneath rippled froth.
She has slipped from the body the sea claimed
And this extremity of water
Is small dew bead impediment
To the heaved love exhaled by the drowned. She knows
History of the sea's excesses must occasionally overspill
With pressures on opposing coasts like Samson's arms.

She speaks harsh syllables to me
Of my neglect. Will not accept
That to exchange words
Equally on terms with
Quantity of sea and
Pitch night surround
Is futile without an
Exigent birth of patience
And a tense cavort with wisdom.
Less which
The necessary humility is crushed –
A shocked turning to cowardice
Then nothing, imagining an ant,
Aware, then dead of an
Overturning pyramid.

Part of the water, like a vein of hers
Follows inland if you turn your back
In an escape attempt.
People know their own rivers.
From birth the smells and noises
Get through the pores. I grow
Impatient of the aimless Thames,
At how this part of her,
Prostituted to the
Carrying of ships which make money,
Remains constant, still tastes salt.
Her tantrums reek of the incommunicable,
Because the image as whole
Revolts at the applying
Of one sector of sea to
Gauge her acritude
With the sleight that
Markets coloured, ordinary
Salts as elixir.

It is the difficulty
Of succumbing – the wrenched effort
Geared to the exact, receptive stature
Required before she gives.
Alternatives are few,
The failed escape, to walk forward
Steadily deeper until drowned.
Or to stand considering the abstract
Against this onslaught
Of pure, unacquired nature,
Our cursed familiar, the
Inadmissible fugitive from
Cold brains swollen with science.

Once in appeasement, maidens were
Offered outside city walls
Or scapegoats devoured.
Today souls are in demand,
These are being eaten slowly.

My loose head,
Rocked in this tight music,
Stayed, not wanting suicide or escape,
There being so much to receive
That I am incapable of accepting.
Minos' ring, cast out,
Would, if it reached bottom,
Make a symbolic marriage of the affair.
But it would probably become
Entangled in fish net
And my meaning be misconstrued.

I pray the abstract becomes me
For I have little else to wear.

RITUAL

Her control over the valley
Was established cruelly
As the least of nature
Suffered without stricture.

Fire over the tarred roads scorched
The bare trees' arched
Limbs grafting berserk
White wounds in their bark.

A tortured bird chaste
In the fabric of its nest,
Violated by flame
Was charred in its fledgling prime.

The crows' distance was severed
From where they hovered;
Slowed wings limp in the lead heat
Dishevelling their black flight.

One boy who young like a god
By wolves had been suckled and laid
Sleeping among earth and leaves
Is quarry as hag eyed she raves

Of betrayal. Grown strong
With milk from the moon's crescent fang
The choir of her anger will force
Him out as victim of the chase.

She could bring the sky down to net
Him but knows her keen axe is right.
Soon his head falls and a new year
Grinds the burst corn of her child's hair.

THE SUSPECT LOVE

I had half the sounds of spring in my head
That night you were mercenary with me
Near Kentish Town.
Dust substantiated the dew over
The Parliament Hill Fields
And I thought of Keats and Dylan Thomas,
How suspect their respective loves became in death.
The one for a woman unmoved,
The other for humanity.

Walking from you towards Camden Town,
Where Thomas had laced the war years with alcohol,
I invited the stillness near the Greek church
To absolve me.
To prevent my committing predatory
Acts in love's cause or conversely
Making false recognition
Of all that was plausible in your eyes.
The light over the grey road seemed purposeful,
Combining sight and sound
To a poise where decisions were possible
Against the nerveless traffic.

Instants have purity beyond analysis.
The moment arms fall relaxed,
Emptied of further loving,
So fall the chisel, pen and brush.
The previous canvas is dead
Like that year passed in Paris
Because it was the thing to do.
Next time new attitudes or diversions
Will be exploited.
Sincerity exists in the created,
The creator goes on differently,
Eager to persuade fresh dimensions from raw clay,
Artist only at the moment of completion.

He knows love in imitation solves nothing.
Most scholars who raise the dead,
Seeking to resolve fundamentals,
Succeed only in breathing frail complexions
On established depths –
Like the wind changing direction through trees.

Before I may name my god
And confer with him
It is necessary to expose
The true qualities of love
And declare the dross as falsehood.
But I learn from shade
Amorphous answers
That force initiative within
The whole self's interplay.

The contest between innocence and the brute
Is, like art, perfected at the second when the rope
Snaps between two ailments at tug of war.
But it is difficult to place the debris.

Occasionally people are good for each other.
With each act of compassion the city
Contracts and the heart expands with
Tolerance to personal, blind complacency that
Condones the suffering,
The sleek schemes worked out in cellars.
Dried tears' salt is indiscernible
To the furred tongues of well being.

Near Mornington Crescent
Ill treatment of a child
Resounds through a basement window.
The method of remonstration
Defeats those who pass and
Again shadow conceals guilt
But more awkwardly than Dartmoor stone.

So, if you turn to me in Kentish Town –
I mean to the marriage bed –
Will our love erect walls to
Shut out pain of the nameless
With whom every day we cross glances.
Keats never tasted his most aching love
Which writhed in his head like goldfish.
Her cold heart preserved it to his tubercular end.
Thomas kept his alive
But whisky proved necessary.
And since domesticity is supposed to quiet the muse,
Will I blame in years some staleness on your ageing hair?

But if we keep the walls from forming,
The light open in the eccentric dark,
The dream virile,
Attainable only in uncertain,
Surprised onslaughts when the words
For it fail or are again different
Yet familiar, without the brash wrench
Of disconnected change or addition,
(Say natural growth,
Free from distortion – the kind
Of agrarian chemicals men spray
And term indoctrination), we may
Find permanently the other half of the sounds
Of spring which, of course, includes the suffering.

REPRISAL

The esoteric rites
Performed in the arteries of cities
Within sealed rooms
Are aftermath of Socrates;
His obsessive refusal to
Admit the nature of the need,
Finding consolation with
The smooth skinned Alcibiades
Or the male, intellectual sun.

Now many veins
Network the distortion
Horizontally to the levelling couch
Where dignity lies grovelling
Like the injured Wilde in Reading.

Think that a cheese, or two eyes, mouth
And nose within a circle will suffice your children?

As reprisal for this lunar caricature,
Semele hides herself
And to those unlucky, tragic men,
Holds up the moon as mirror to the sun
Where independent of the female
They watch their image watching themselves.

And love awkwardly, like limbs and bodies,
With malignant passion –
Sure prelude to degeneration –
Unnaturally deprived of the origins of homage.

SECTION 2   *Personal and positional*

INITIATION

The sick flowers
Hide beneath
Corpses of leaves,
Brittle veined
In brown,
Crumbling to earth for
The soil's renewal.

This sense of pause
Is gentleness
In still life –
The image of
The mother whose hands
Ache to run over
Her unborn child,
Deterred forcibly
Until the womb
Sees fit to
Yield it for her arms.

There is
A similar time
Allowed all men
When growth is
Still as God.
Care and the
Delicacy required
For its handling
Centre at this
Inaction.

The younger the
Innocence involved
The more
Rigorously it
Learns the
Depth, colour and
Authenticity
Of the slightest
Falsehood that this
May be named
And thus diminished.

The woman
Triangular with
Child waits out
This process of
Initiation,
First distinguishing
Then aware of
Her supremacy
Over the lies
Necessary to
Normality or
The various labels
Tagged on the
Habit of compromise.

Having this reason
To live
Allows no must
Of stale untruth
Over her being.
It rots like the
Shed leaves to
Nourish a new
Innocence.

Yield this child
Soon into her arms.
The illness of flowers
Deserves birth.
The cure is to
Reject light usage
Of the word 'love'.

THE FATALITY

Those who stare at demolition,
The road hole, or the gigantic birth
Within the scaffold cage midwifed by
An erect, surprisingly agile crane,
Also gather, vacantly anonymous,
Round the casualty, head pillowed
On a raincoat, obstructing the pavement.

Personal animation is repressed to the minimum.
Participation inadmissible because
The victim, the stretched mutilation,
Might tomorrow be contained in other clothes
That now shift awkwardly, the wearer
Conscious of his preserved self.

After the ambulance, the slow drift
Back with whatever the mind was previously
Occupied. But the tension lasts
Until the dregs of vivid blood, smudged by sand,
Are suddenly inconspicuous or
Love's detritus is scraped from underfoot.
Always the traces of fatality
Disappear quickly by unidentifiable means.

Soon others, oblivious, accepting the risk,
Crowd the island from which he, expecting mainlands,
Stepped to a normal, pedestrian death.

MAHLER

Arranging the manifestation in its
Correct posture along the fluted vibrato
Of a strained horn is like
Training an oak branch to be supple
As clematis over a trellis;
A portent that nature might snap
Under his brutal scrutiny.

The human complexity of
Imagining death's simplicity
With faith's frailty or the atheist's aplomb
Necessitates collusion of contrasts.

A child runs from its parents' quarrel,
Is jerked like a hooked fish
On the ridiculous hilarity of a churned organ
Abruptly displacing and emphasizing tragedy.
While Core's mother wept
Elsewhere the idiot Pan pranced,
Confusing in one vision
The farewell and the burlesque.

To feel the act of time is to foretaste
The agony without which joy is banal;
To anticipate the death that, advertised,
Slips from its hoarding to find pain
Has already invaded the flowers
Rescued by Chinese hands
From decaying songs in the earth.

    The air is fired with sea.
    Eels writhe in melting salt,
    Their backbones small flagellations
    In the detail of heaving water.
    On shore rejected meat rots,
    Falls from a whale's ruined structure
    Like dried leather sloughed from a book's spine.
    The wind strings the skeleton
    And the ribbed, original harp
    Frays with torn music –
    Bronze presages pointing
    Through death's silver future desolations
    That pied history has since named.

But there is relief in the rustic holiday.
Corn bleaches a crystal respite
In the dusk's appraisal
Of one day's achievements,
As the labourer who fingers
The keys of an evening harmonium.

The fluid evolution of the hymn
Drapes the senses with the cool blur
Of storm rain on a window
Obscuring tree shapes of warm green.
The dry, down walking fly can
Afford leisure between room and rain,
Segregated from muscular weather.

Though true experience seems
Interminable its
Recollection is like that
Of a brief communion.
Even with the immeasurable
Extent of a growing love,
Because there is no end
There is no way of saying 'goodbye'.
In school, when a boy is told
To fetch a book from another room
His return is never doubted.

The first cell of stirring, creative
Energy draws its life from the mind
That doubts routine, accepted certainties.
It matures, there is short life,
Some time for work,
Until from soil nebulous with past flesh
Speech filters through dry cavities.
The carline voice of Persephone,
No longer seductive,
Calls home all images against their will.

TENEMENT WORKSHOP

Fumes had gathered in the room
Because, overwhelmed by a line of music's
Effrontery to stay ungrasped,
I had been careless with the fire.
Opening the window cleared things
A little, except for the tension.
I envied those accomplished with words
The relief of the arguable.

This place reminds me of a screen set
Thrown up on the cheap
With signs of temperament and eccentricity –
The star's heel marks on the floor
Where she dug in
Petulantly, craving more camera or profile.
I imagine her beautiful,
I have to see it that way
Believing that love or work
However trivial
Requires a muse of vocation.

Holding the instrument's stem felt good.
But there had been complaints about the noise,
So now I blow gently,
Fingering with no reed to sound
And be branded as nuisance,
My theme by its silence
Even the less articulate
And therefore unarguable.

The discarded sequences are real
In that unvoiced, they will not cease to exist
While so many muffle their music,
A reed or bow lying on the table,
Forced aside like the nature we had once
Of doing things for love alone.

NOT FOR MY DAUGHTER'S EARS

The inhuman acts, the lament
Of creation, the suffering
Of the created, no less the blunt
Words that perhaps killed a channel
Of feeling precious to child or adult,
Shrugged off, now fix me rigidly.
My own murders are numbered,
Filed carefully in a room
Set off from my averted eyes.
I am at one with the offender who
Avoids the expected places,
Knowing the official awaits to
Serve a writ. So long he
Succeeds but the police
Come and his case is out,
Though never in quite the context he
Imagined. Always it seems he is
Daubed worse, the injustice
Exaggerated unjustly — his
Reason an unacceptable excuse.

Gross attempts at love,
Clumsy with criminal indelicacy,
Although necessary are now
Seen for what they were.
You may watch the climber,
Large with intrusive scenery,
Grow smaller, the humps of his surroundings
Ironed smooth with altitude.
From solitary peak he
Views the true perspective of what he
Befriended or grappled with as
Victuals of his upward crawl.
Love when attained, like peace,
Is hardest to maintain.
I have been granted the love which
Presented her, but its learning
Is not for my daughter's ears.

EXCURSION

The night is educated to the grief sustained
By two inept criers for love, unmarked
Whereas my face is day scarred.

Her dress is ecstatic with momentary moons.
He kneels and with that first, distant Elizabeth's
Grace, a prayer knights him.

They achieve the unreasonable in bed
From which all imperfect labour is withdrawn,
Exposing this unforced, mental flower.

To show them by day the exact room, its rough deal
Corners, folding chair, sagged, grey sheeted bed,
Would surely undeceive them?

I called, and while they heard me out I noticed her
Rheumatic arm which had earlier conferred
Some strange nobility on his rounded back.

But they called me harsh names despite the shield
Of reality I offered them to keep the dreams off,
And they turned away still hand in frail hand.

SECTION 3   *The action of discipline*

SIX CONTEMPORARY ALLUSIONS

I   If to be accused in art of a lack
     Of attendance to the cause of rustic

     Simplicity is like being goaded
     By offspring, gauche and worldly persuaded

     Who inherit the gift of rejecting
     Painful deliberations, inflicting

     Right and wrong, accepting either with ease,
     This is emulation of the last phase.

II   The son sows what he reaps since he exhales
     In line the bad breath of Eden reptiles.

     If sin is depicted as the start, what
     Chance to rise above a secular tart?

III   The heart's ventricles are bulbous with hot
     Blood pumping because of a first train set

     That riles the boy by jumping the sharp curves.
     In that small scale world the magnified shoves

     Are presages of how greed will evolve.
     Oaths sustain and sex is a safety valve.

IV   He must also learn to distinguish all
     Prevention measures, including the pill.

     (This is very important because birth,
     Death and religion acknowledge one truth

     In common – multiplication. There is
     More of each than ever before. Appraise

     Semantics, bombs and communications
     Respectively, the three primed relations).

     Homage to the male is the woman's task,
     She swallows the pill with a cancer risk.

V In Summer when heat steams up my glasses,
  Spare me the benefit of your tresses.

  We lie in the sun on the slope failing
  To see that love is the most beguiling,

  Most missed because most obvious fragrance.
  I spend my life with you in ignorance.

  Let me draw the poison from that old hurt,
  Then stretch and wear your limbs like a new suit.

VI Calmer now I see the corn is not green.
  It is ripe and it is time that the grain

  Was gathered. But not by me, I have passed
  The stage where anything so useful pressed

  Me into activity. There is no
  Need – always the wind can get up and go.

A RITUAL FOR HOUSE WARMING

First you should arrange these bare rooms
With furniture and casual articles
That will let slip some of your whims
And rouse curiosity. Too many clues
Will dispel interest, for homes,
Like people, can be seen through and the locals
Are always suspicious. Like gnomes
Of reconnaissance, they stare from bicycles,

Eager to judge, dismiss, condemn,
Write abroad about with the promise of more
To divulge – the lid off in ten
Helpings with morsels they deduce to the fore.
Confused you might be forgiven
Should you turn the vicar away from the door
Because upheaval in your den
Has disfigured every square inch of free floor.

Then when you are straight and they call
You may like one or two. But be sure no-one
Will have noticed that book title
You propped blatantly under the Mondrian
They credited you with. Vital
Here to be rigid and, evading return
Invitations, to remain still
Distant but unflinchingly deep and benign.

This countenance may see you through,
But as a last resort discuss the merits
Of Vivaldi which concern you
Fundamentally. Ill-mentioned favourites
Like the Beatles must be seen through
As finished and some obscure jester of sorts
Be crushed for an obscene debut
Which stupified establishment habitats.

–Accept the honey as if Miss
Jones and not her staid bees were responsible.
And be sure you neither dismiss
Nor ban aesthetically from your table
One whose surly hackles would rise
At denial, branding you despicable
Poseur, who then, in journalese,
Proves artists, unlike houses, expendable.

THE SLEEPER AND THE BEAST

Closely with hose of coarse
Texture, the stiff lids clamp
Vision between repose
And the harsh, metal lamp
That gravels the worn eyes.

The beast in the room lives
Its term of hours unnerved
By the deep architraves
Of the skull where, deprived
Of access it disproves

The mind's immunity
By penetrating flesh.
Joined in disparity
Blood warmth pricks the pores' mesh
To vivid unity

Of pain like parchment drawn
Taut over the sleeper.
And the movement is torn
Back as agues taper
From nightmare to dream. Wan

The figure wakes, ashen
At what its sleep unleashed
From the body's lesion,
As the beast, replenished,
Spurns further adhesion.

DIARY BETWEEN MARRIAGES

The oblique entries are stern,
Immaculate, often self sufficient
In their mastery of order. Deficient
Love, void of any small return
I might give, however free from disdain.

The month was April. Year fifty three.
A marriage failing hopelessly.
Two people dogmeat to each other
Sustained with nerves, cooled by the lather
Of oaths spat back in grind mawkishly.

The release four years later was advent
Of nothing except fear of a repeat
Debasement. Maturing in defeat
I next craved cold women who were distant
Enough for respite while lust was latent.

I persisted with things that reversed
On me. Got used to being divorced.
Small grace from unexpected directions
Surprised me often, though reflections
Of self pity were not too soon displaced.

I am not ashamed of my come back
Or the way it seemed an accident.
Learning to feel became an implement
I used in love to discard its fake
Voices. My darling reads the noise I make.

SAPPHO AND THE UNGAINLY TUTOR

His slow grasp of metaphors
Unhinged him. The rudiments
Of farce clung like sophomores
Ridiculing evidence

That he, forty years life screened,
Had roped off and remoulded
To theories now judged unsound.
Pride, his pet bull was gelded.

There was a rumour that love
Had disowned him when he read
Fear in the eyes of a live
Sappho estranged in his bed.

He would distort to create
And this jagged reversion
On her small body, despite
His tenderness, was fusion

Of contempt and desire to
Exact response through the mail
Of her skin. Incognito
His untried lust, prehensile

With claws, stripped her capricious
Flesh raw of its blanketing
Against such thrust, in raucous
Climax of strength abating.

White hands in the morning grip
Mirrors in rooms where pain was
Anchored to perversion. Sheep-
Like he dresses, shaves and goes

Back to his faculty of
Ill cut theories, believing
That harsh prose will reveal love
At the core of his grieving.

This ungainly theft supplants
The pleasure that made her slope
Of breasts a secure cadence
For his metaphor for sleep,

And wakeful, the night turns her
Body into ice – the black
Kind that shrinks the mind, colder
Now because the act was fake.

THE LEAST OF GENTLENESS

Prone to the hygienic sound
(The shrill edge of a lark
Cleaning the air from its freak
Stance, like a reprimand,

Poised in its strung atmosphere
Devoid of gravity),
The crucial and inmost fear
Is steel's virginity

Tempered in the surgeon's knife.
If the flesh could condone
Stitched penetrations as proof
Against growth of mundane

Cancers that drain the substance
In the keen acumen
Of a wholesome dissonance,
Scars and the bitumen

They weep would knit to atone
For this just violence.
But the rape near the breastbone
Augurs the imminence

Of operation shock – will
Dragging constitution
Through the heart machine; the stale,
Second hand transfusion.

Grey in the white sheets, flesh strains
Toward recovery.
The stomach contracts its chains
Of nerves as every

Move is observed and charted.
Prowess of body passed
Slyly when what was rooted
Was removed with the least

Of gentleness and utmost
Skill. Released with this mark
Beneath dayclothes, pray the lark
Has also fouled its nest.

CAGE

They attached instruments to her head
Presuming disorder of the mind
Which, in its disquiet, upended
And panicked like an ostrich for sand.

The regulated stabs of current
Cut her thoughtflow to fragments, detached
Like timber from tall pines, inherent,
Yet sawn separate, trimmed and dispatched –

Put together again cleanly, purged
Of imperfection. But the mind plays
It tough, refusing to be assuaged
By electric antedotes. It shies

From shock activity and the masked
Avarice for experiment deep
In their rehearsals of pain, their frisked
Countenances permitting no shape

To foreshadow the patient's dog eyed
Apprehension. From varied postures
Of subordination thoughts upbraid
The doctors' arrogance with gestures,

Half completed, that will culminate
In spite on the unfortunate nurse.
Whispers of plots to eliminate
The insane bid her anger disperse

And soon, birdlike with timidity,
She flutters under the next white coat
For warm wing shelter, humility
Snug in the smell of a man's armpit.

She will leave soon, part cured, less haggard,
But more lean than her wan flesh implies.
That her images are haphazard
And less meaningful exemplifies

The patched, intermittent memory,
Purposely shattered, now left to her
To repair forcibly – if this wry
Freedom to construct does not deter.

THE DEMONSTRATORS

We reached out for the shreds of tyres
Left where hot wheels had strained at the ground –
Grains stripped from the burnt rubber pores,
The weak entrails such tension had spurned.

Black segments in our hands like grit
As we moved over the road and stooped
Low above the asphalt to grate
The palm's smooth flesh on its surface, sloped

Upwards to a ridge-like centre.
In the end we lay on the far verge,
Glad of the moist grass to counter
Our skin's dry graze with its soft massage.

We could have been crawling, wounded
But spared, from a metal contortion
Of crashed cars or crouching winded
From a maniac's concentration

Of small arms fire intent upon
A miniature massacre. We might
Have come through keeping our heads down
And elbows in as we had been taught

When the police broke up meetings
From horseback and we ran for cover.
But a patrol from the joustings
Elsewhere came on us without favour

Of preliminaries and dragged
Us in. Hands rough from the road we were
Examined for pox, presumed drugged,
Then abandoned in a room stripped bare

Of furniture for questioning.
Guests of brutality make the most
Of their respite and surfacing
From the mire, we reared against the beast

By kissing beneath the spyhole.
Releasing us, our patron state bends
Backwards – but we shall grow servile,
It is too easy to have clean hands.

CROW'S FALL

The crow's foot punctured the stained glass
As the hurled bird struck the buttress.

Wind crashed against stone the sightless
Wrap of its warm, limp winged carcass.

Falling into like black it scraped
Mortar from arms that were flesh stripped.

As earth broke over its slight head
The beak point rasped against fluted

Rock poised towards the impetus
Of its feathered dive. The foetus

Of its fall was the tracked angle
That froze downwards from this single

Malevolence; how the captured
Motion lunged as its breath expired.

When night jars on fatal nature,
Coercing darkness to secure

This bird with each bone so fractured,
Flesh so jellied that each sectored

Throb stills, creation is revealed
As stark labour of cells entailed

In intricate, arduous craft.
But at birth the fledgling is left

With loss of interest to whims
Of elements, disease and worms.

They replaced the glass from beneath
The buttress – an act of half truth,

Deep from which stress drove the dark bird
Like a maxim that somehow strayed

From its claw holes or grip on life
That slipped, leaving no trace nor grief.

*This first edition has been designed,
printed & published by Cape Goliard Press,
10a Fairhazel Gardens, London N.W.6,
& of this edition 50 have been signed &
numbered by the author.*

Title-page illustration by Heinke Jenkins.

Printed in Great Britain.